Caitlin Clark

Basketball's Revolutionary Force

Darrin E. Jones

Caitlin Clark

Copyright © 2025 by Darrin E. Jones

All rights reserved. No part of this publication may be replicated, disseminated, or transmitted in any form or by any means, including photocopying, recording, or other electronic or mechanical methods, without the prior written consent of the publisher, except in the case of brief excerpts embodied in critical reviews and specific other noncommercial uses permitted by copyright law.

Caitlin Clark

Contents

Introduction

Born to Compete – The West Des Moines Prodigy

The Rise of a Scoring Phenom – Dominating Dowling Catholic

Choosing Home – Committing to the Iowa Hawkeyes

Instant Impact – A Freshman Star is Born

The Face of the Game – Transforming Women's College Basketball

Caitlin Clark

Rivalries, Records, and Rewriting History

The Cultural Phenomenon – Beyond the Court

Senior Season and the National Spotlight

Going Pro – WNBA and the Next Chapter

Legacy in Motion – Caitlin Clark's Lasting Impact

Conclusion

Caitlin Clark

Introduction

In an era when athletes are measured not just by their stats but by their ability to shake the ground beneath them, Caitlin Clark didn't just step onto the basketball court—she stormed it.

Before the packed arenas, the record-shattering highlights, and the millions of eyes glued to her every move, she was just a girl from West Des Moines with a fiery spirit and a ball in her hands. But what Caitlin carried with her every time she laced up her sneakers was something far greater than just talent—it was the purpose. A purpose to change the game.

Caitlin Clark

She didn't ask to be a revolutionary. She just played like one.

Clark's game was unlike anything women's basketball had ever seen. Deep three-pointers taken without hesitation. Dazzling passes that threaded through defenders like poetry in motion. A competitive drive that could outmatch seasoned pros. She had the kind of flair and fearless style that drew comparisons to legends across the sport, but make no mistake—Caitlin Clark was carving her own path, not following in anyone else's footsteps.

This wasn't just about basketball. This was about momentum. Movement. A visible shift in how the world viewed women's sports. Caitlin didn't ask for attention—her play demanded it. And as she climbed the all-time scoring ranks,

Caitlin Clark

battled elite opponents on national stages, and captivated audiences from coast to coast, she became something more than just an athlete. She became a symbol of what was possible.

This book is not just the story of her statistics, trophies, or viral moments—though there are plenty of those. It's the story of a girl who believed in herself before the world knew her name. It's the story of a player who stayed home to build something bigger than herself. It's the story of resilience, grit, and grace under pressure.

Caitlin Clark: Basketball's Revolutionary Force invites you behind the curtain—into the gyms where her legend was born, the locker rooms where her leadership took root, and the spotlight

Caitlin Clark

where she grew from a prodigy to a cultural icon. Through ten gripping chapters, we'll trace her meteoric rise from high school phenom to college superstar to WNBA game-changer.

This isn't just a biography. It's a celebration of change.

Because every generation gets a player who redefines what's possible. And for this one, her name is Caitlin Clark.

Caitlin Clark

1: Born to Compete – The West Des Moines Prodigy

The backyard basketball hoop at the Clark family home in West Des Moines had seen better days. Its weathered backboard bore the scars of thousands of shots, the rim slightly bent from countless dunks attempted by siblings determined to outdo one another. For young Caitlin Clark, this unassuming hoop wasn't just playground equipment—it was her first arena.

On summer evenings, as golden light filtered through Iowa oak trees, nine-year-old Caitlin would challenge her older brothers to games of H-O-R-S-E or one-on-one, refusing to quit until

Caitlin Clark

darkness made it impossible to see the ball. The neighbors grew accustomed to the rhythmic thump of dribbling and the occasional shouts of triumph or frustration echoing down Ashworth Road. What they couldn't have known was that they were witnessing the earliest chapters of a basketball revolution.

"Caitlin never wanted to come inside," her mother Anne would later recall with a laugh. "We'd call her for dinner, and she'd negotiate for 'just five more shots.' Those five shots always turned into twenty."

Born in January 2002, Caitlin was the middle child in a household where athletics wasn't just encouraged—it was a way of life. Her father Brent had played baseball at Simpson College,

Caitlin Clark

while her brothers Blake and Colin were accomplished multi-sport athletes in their own right. In this family, competitive fire wasn't taught; it was inherited, as natural as breathing.

The Clarks' dining table often transformed into an extension of the playing field, with dinnertime conversations erupting into spirited debates about games, players, and strategies. Even board games turned fierce. Anne once found young Caitlin in tears after losing at Monopoly—not because she was a poor sport, but because her competitive spirit burned so intensely.

"She didn't cry because she lost," Brent explained. "She cried because she hadn't figured out how to win yet."

Caitlin Clark

That determination revealed itself early on in local courts. When Caitlin joined her first organized basketball team at age seven, coaches immediately noticed something different about the ponytailed girl who played with an intensity beyond her years. While other children timidly passed the ball away, Caitlin wanted it in her hands when it mattered most.

By fourth grade, she was playing up with older girls. By fifth, she was dominating them. Local youth coaches traded stories about the Clark girl who could shoot from anywhere and seemed to see passes before they happened. At Kingdom Hoops, the prestigious basketball academy in Des Moines, director Jake Sullivan recognized

Caitlin Clark

rare talent when eleven-year-old Caitlin walked through the doors.

"Some kids have skill. Some have basketball IQ. Some have that competitive edge," Sullivan said. "Caitlin had the whole package, and she hadn't even hit middle school."

What set young Caitlin apart wasn't just natural ability. While her peers played seasonally, she lived in the gym year-round. Winter mornings found her arriving at practice an hour early, working on ball-handling drills in an empty gymnasium, the squeak of her shoes on hardwood the only sound bouncing off cinder block walls. Summer days meant shooting sessions where she wouldn't leave until she had made 500 shots—not taken, made.

Caitlin Clark

West Des Moines wasn't a basketball hotbed by national standards, but Iowa's deep-rooted basketball culture provided fertile ground for Clark's budding talents. The state that had embraced girls' six-on-six basketball long before Title IX was the perfect incubator for a young player with outsized dreams. Weekend tournaments across the Midwest became the family routine, the Clark's SUV racking up thousands of miles as they crisscrossed Iowa's highways.

These journeys revealed another side of Caitlin—her encyclopedic knowledge of the game. While other kids dozed off in backseats, she devoured game footage on her iPad, studying the footwork of NBA stars and the

Caitlin Clark

shooting forms of WNBA greats with equal fascination. Her bedroom walls featured posters of Maya Moore and Steph Curry alongside Iowa Hawkeyes memorabilia—a visual prophecy of the worlds she would one day bridge.

Multi-sport excellence marked her early athletic career. She excelled at soccer, displaying the same court vision on the pitch that would later become her basketball trademark. Track and volleyball showcased her overall athleticism. But basketball—basketball was different. On the court, Caitlin wasn't just playing; she was orchestrating, calculating, creating.

"Even at twelve years old, she processed the game differently," remembered her first AAU coach, Mark Miller. "She'd make a pass, and I'd

Caitlin Clark

think, 'Where is she going with that?' Then three seconds later, the play would develop exactly as she'd envisioned it."By eighth grade, college coaches were already taking notice. The girl from West Des Moines was developing a reputation that extended far beyond Iowa's borders. Videos of her no-look passes and logo-distance three-pointers began circulating among coaching staffs. A whisper campaign started: Have you seen the Clark kid from Iowa?

As middle school gave way to high school, Caitlin stood at the threshold of a new challenge. The backyard hoop that had witnessed her earliest dreams would soon be replaced by the gymnasium lights of Dowling Catholic High School. The ponytailed girl with the wicked crossover and fearless shooting range was about

Caitlin Clark

to step onto a bigger stage, bringing with her a competitive fire that would eventually burn bright enough to transform women's basketball forever.Little did the basketball world know that the scoring phenom from Dowling Catholic was about to rewrite what was possible for a high school player in Iowa—and beyond.

Caitlin Clark

2: The Rise of a Scoring Phenom – Dominating Dowling Catholic

The green and gold hallways of Dowling Catholic High School had seen their share of talented athletes over the decades, but nothing could have prepared the West Des Moines institution for the whirlwind that was Caitlin Clark. On the first day of freshman basketball tryouts in 2016, veteran coach Kristin Meyer watched with quiet amazement as the lanky fourteen-year-old with the confident swagger effortlessly outplayed seniors who had been varsity starters for years.

Caitlin Clark

"I'd heard the rumors, of course," Meyer would later recall. "Everyone in Iowa basketball circles was talking about her. But seeing is believing, and what I saw that day was unlike anything I'd encountered in twenty years of coaching."

What Meyer witnessed wasn't just skill—it was a preternatural understanding of basketball's geometric possibilities, packaged in a freshman who looked more comfortable with a ball in her hands than most people feel in their own living rooms. Caitlin made the varsity team not just as a player, but as an immediate starter and the team's offensive centerpiece. The torch hadn't been passed; it had been seized.

Her debut game for the Dowling Catholic Maroons announced her arrival with thunderous

Caitlin Clark

clarity. Facing crosstown rival Valley High School, freshman Clark dropped 27 points, including five three-pointers from distances that made opposing coaches grimace. The local Des Moines Register's modest preview of "promising freshman Caitlin Clark" suddenly seemed like dramatic understatement.

By mid-season, opposing teams were designing entire defensive schemes specifically to contain her. Box-and-ones, double teams, face-guarding—nothing worked consistently. Caitlin possessed that rarest of athletic gifts: the ability to impose her will on a game regardless of the defensive attention thrown her way. When teams played off her, she launched logo threes. When they pressured her, she drove past defenders with a devastating first step. When

Caitlin Clark

help came, she found open teammates with passes of surgical precision.

"Defending Caitlin wasn't like defending a normal high school player," remembered Ankeny High coach Dru McAnelly. "You'd think you had her contained, and suddenly she's pulling up from 30 feet and swishing it. There was no defensive blueprint for that."

Her sophomore season brought new dimensions to her game and new heights to her reputation. Now standing nearly six feet tall, with improved strength and even sharper court vision, Caitlin averaged 27.1 points per game while adding 6.8 assists and 5.4 rebounds. College coaches were no longer just interested—they were infatuated. Practice sessions at Dowling regularly featured Division I coaches lining the walls, clipboards in

Caitlin Clark

hand, expressions oscillating between disbelief and desire.

Notre Dame's Muffet McGraw made personal visits. UConn's Geno Auriemma called regularly. Oregon, Duke, Texas—the bluebloods of women's college basketball all envisioned Clark as their program's cornerstone. Meanwhile, Iowa's Lisa Bluder quietly laid groundwork closer to home, attending games without fanfare, building a relationship rooted in authenticity rather than spectacle.

As the scholarship offers multiplied, Caitlin remained remarkably centered. Teammates marveled at her ability to compartmentalize the growing circus around her recruitment. "She'd have just finished a phone call with some

Caitlin Clark

legendary coach," remembered teammate Ella Hardy, "and five minutes later she'd be helping me with my math homework like nothing had happened."

Junior year transformed Clark from Iowa phenomenon to national sensation. Her scoring average jumped to 32.6 points per game, with highlight packages regularly featuring shots from distances that made basketball purists question both her judgment and their own eyes—until the ball swished through the net with infuriating consistency. A 45-point performance against top-ranked Waukee went viral when she hit a game-winning three from just inside half court. ESPN included the shot on its Top 10 Plays—rare territory for a girls' high school basketball player.

Caitlin Clark

"I've never understood why people are so surprised when I shoot from far out," Caitlin told a local reporter with characteristic confidence. "I practice those shots every day. They're not lucky when they go in."

The Maroons reached the state tournament that year, with Clark scoring 42 points in a heartbreaking semifinal loss. As she walked off the court, the entire Veterans Memorial Auditorium rose in standing ovation—a rare moment of unanimity between opposing fans who recognized they were witnessing something extraordinary.

By senior year, Caitlin Clark games became events that transcended high school basketball. Dowling's gymnasium consistently sold out, with tickets being scalped online—a first for

Caitlin Clark

Iowa girls' basketball. College coaches had largely accepted they were watching a future pro. NBA players occasionally appeared courtside, drawn by rumors of the girl who played with a style reminiscent of Steph Curry.

Clark's senior campaign was a masterclass in offensive basketball. She averaged an astounding 37.3 points per game while shooting 46% from three-point range—numbers that seemed plucked from a video game rather than actual box scores. Her 53-point explosion against Southeast Polk included ten three-pointers, most from well beyond the arc, cementing her reputation as perhaps the greatest scorer in Iowa high school history.

Caitlin Clark

National awards and recognitions accumulated: McDonald's All-American, Gatorade Player of the Year finalist, Jordan Brand Classic selectee. But what those accolades couldn't capture was how Caitlin had transformed Iowa girls' basketball into appointment viewing, how she'd made young girls across the Midwest believe that basketball greatness wasn't just for boys or coastal phenoms.

As her storied high school career wound down, the question on everyone's mind shifted from "How good is she?" to "Where will she go?" The basketball world held its breath as Caitlin Clark, now the most coveted recruit in America, prepared to make her college decision. The girl who had rewritten scoring records and expectations at Dowling Catholic was about to

Caitlin Clark

make a choice that would send shockwaves through women's college basketball—a decision that would keep her closer to home than many expected, and set the stage for a collegiate career that would transcend the sport itself.

Caitlin Clark

3: Choosing Home – Committing to the Iowa Hawkeyes

November in Iowa brings a particular kind of quiet—cornfields stripped bare, early darkness settling over towns, and a certain stillness that precedes winter. But on November 8, 2019, the atmosphere in the Dowling Catholic gymnasium crackled with anticipation. Reporters jostled for position, cameras flashed, and family members dabbed at proud tears as Caitlin Clark, the most coveted women's basketball recruit in America, approached the microphone.

Caitlin Clark

Three hats sat on the table before her: Notre Dame's navy and gold, Duke's royal blue, and Iowa's black and gold. The basketball world had been speculating for months. Would she choose the championship pedigree of Notre Dame? The academic prestige of Duke? Or would she do the unthinkable and stay home, selecting an Iowa program that hadn't reached a Final Four in decades?

Caitlin paused, her expression unreadable. Then, with the confident half-smile that had become her trademark, she reached for the black and gold cap and placed it squarely on her head.

"I'm staying home," she announced, her voice steady despite the emotion of the moment. "I'll be playing for the Iowa Hawkeyes."

Caitlin Clark

The gymnasium erupted. In living rooms across Iowa, fans who had watched her development through four remarkable high school seasons celebrated a decision that defied conventional basketball wisdom. Top recruits typically flocked to established powerhouses—UConn, Stanford, Notre Dame, South Carolina. Iowa was respected but hadn't been considered elite in women's basketball for years. Caitlin Clark had just changed that equation with five simple words.

The decision had not come easily or quickly. For months, some of women's basketball's most legendary coaches had made impassioned pitches in the Clark family living room. Muffet McGraw of Notre Dame presented a vision of

Caitlin Clark

Clark leading the Irish to multiple championships. Duke offered academic excellence paired with ACC competition. UConn's Geno Auriemma, winner of eleven national titles, had made his interest clear. Each pitch came with impeccable credentials and promises of national visibility.

"Everyone assumed I'd leave," Caitlin later reflected. "That's what the top recruits usually do. They go to the programs that have already won multiple championships. But something about building something special where I grew up just felt right."

Behind her decision stood Iowa head coach Lisa Bluder, whose approach to recruitment had been refreshingly different. While other coaches had

Caitlin Clark

dazzled with presentation, Bluder had connected with authenticity. She hadn't promised championships or guaranteed starting spots—she had offered partnership, a system that would maximize Clark's unique talents, and a chance to elevate women's basketball in her home state.

"Coach Bluder never tried to sell me on Iowa," Clark explained. "She showed me how we could build something together. There's a difference."

The relationship between Bladder and Clark had developed gradually over years. The veteran coach had attended Caitlin's games since middle school, not with fanfare or an entourage, but often alone, sitting quietly in corner bleachers. What she saw was not just a scoring phenom but a basketball intellect that matched her own.

Caitlin Clark

"Some players you have to teach your system to," Bluder would later say. "With Caitlin, I knew immediately we would expand our system together."

In the weeks following her commitment, Clark's decision reverberated through women's basketball. ESPN analysts debated whether she had made a mistake bypassing traditional powers. Recruiting experts questioned whether Iowa could surround her with enough talent to compete nationally. Meanwhile, season ticket sales for Iowa women's basketball surged, with the athletic department reporting a 40% increase within days of her announcement.

What outsiders didn't understand was that Clark's choice reflected deeper values than mere

Caitlin Clark

basketball calculation. Growing up in West Des Moines, she had watched Iowa Hawkeye games with her family since childhood. She had attended camps at Carver-Hawkeye Arena, where her father would someday watch her play from section JJ, row 27. The familiar drive along Interstate 80 from Des Moines to Iowa City—just under two hours of flat highway flanked by farmland—had been part of her life's geography forever.

"Home isn't just a place," Caitlin explained to a local reporter asking about her decision. "It's the people who know you, who've supported you before you were anybody special. Iowa supported girls' basketball when nobody else did. That matters."

Caitlin Clark

Her commitment transformed Iowa women's basketball overnight. Fellow recruits who might have overlooked the program suddenly showed interest in joining Clark in Iowa City. Coaching staff around the Big Ten began strategizing for the Clark era years before she would play her first collegiate game. Hawkeye fans, known for their passionate support of wrestling and football, began purchasing women's basketball tickets in unprecedented numbers.

In the months between her commitment and high school graduation, Clark continued dominating at Dowling Catholic, unfazed by the growing expectations that now shadowed her. When COVID-19 disrupted her senior season, she adapted, organizing impromptu workouts and shooting sessions in empty parks and driveways.

Caitlin Clark

By the time she collected her diploma in spring 2020, the weight of an entire state's basketball hopes rested on her shoulders.

That summer, as she prepared for the transition to collegiate athlete, Clark maintained the grueling training regimen that had defined her youth—600 shots every morning, ball-handling drills until her fingers ached, conditioning work that left her gasping on gymnasium floors. But now she added film study of Iowa's offensive sets, determined to arrive on campus ready to contribute immediately.

What nobody could have predicted, though, was just how immediate and transformative that contribution would be. When Caitlin Clark finally donned the black and gold uniform and

Caitlin Clark

stepped onto the court at Carver-Hawkeye Arena in November 2020, she wasn't just beginning her collegiate career—she was igniting a revolution in women's basketball that would transcend her sport. The freshman from West Des Moines was about to announce herself to the nation in spectacular fashion, with a debut season that would leave the basketball world scrambling for superlatives and reaching for record books.

Caitlin Clark

4: Instant Impact – A Freshman Star is Born

The squeak of basketball shoes on hardwood echoed through a nearly empty Carver-Hawkeye Arena on November 25, 2020. COVID-19 protocols had transformed what should have been a raucous college debut into something eerily quiet—15,000 seats vacant except for a smattering of cardboard cutouts and staff. As Iowa prepared to face Northern Iowa in their season opener, the basketball world wondered: Would Caitlin Clark's game translate immediately to the collegiate level, or would she need time to adjust?

Caitlin Clark

They didn't wander long.

Three minutes into her collegiate career, Clark pulled up from 26 feet—a distance that would make NBA players hesitate—and launched. The ball rotated perfectly, splashing through the net with a satisfying snap. On Iowa's next possession, she drove past two defenders for an acrobatic layup. Minutes later, she threaded a no-look pass through traffic for an easy assist. By halftime, she had 17 points.

"I remember thinking, 'This isn't normal,'" Iowa assistant coach Jan Jensen would later recall. "Freshmen aren't supposed to look this comfortable this quickly. She played like she'd been in our program for years."

Caitlin Clark

The final stat line—27 points, 8 rebounds, 4 assists—announced Clark's arrival with thunderous clarity. But those who had watched closely saw something beyond numbers: a freshman who played with the swagger of a senior All-American, who operated with a green light that Coach Lisa Bluder had never before granted a first-year player.

That debut proved to be no fluke. Against Drake University in her second game, Clark erupted for 30 points. Against Iowa State, Iowa's bitter in-state rival, she delivered 34 points and 7 assists in a statement victory. By Christmas, the basketball world was buzzing about the freshman from Des Moines who played with a fearlessness rarely seen in the women's college game."She pulls up from distances that make no

Caitlin Clark

mathematical sense," wrote ESPN's Charlie Creme after watching Clark drain three consecutive shots from beyond 30 feet against Michigan. "And yet, for her, they're good shots. She's redefining what's possible."

What separates extraordinary athletes from merely great ones isn't just ability but audacity—the willingness to attempt what others consider impossible. Clark possessed this quality in abundance. Her range extended to midcourt, her passes found windows that didn't appear to exist, and her confidence never wavered, even when shots didn't fall.

By January 2021, opposing coaches were designing entire defensive schemes specifically to contain her. Box-and-ones, full-court pressure,

Caitlin Clark

physical denials—nothing worked consistently. Against Northwestern, facing constant double-teams, Clark scored 33 points with 13 assists. Against Minnesota, she poured in 37 points with a Big Ten freshman-record 11 three-pointers."We tried everything," lamented Minnesota coach Lindsay Whalen. "We face-guarded her, we trapped her, we pushed her to her left. Nothing mattered. Great players make coaches look like they don't know what they're doing."What made Clark's freshman campaign all the more remarkable was the backdrop against which it unfolded. The COVID-19 pandemic had transformed college athletics. Teams played in empty arenas, faced constant testing, endured paused seasons and quarantines. For many freshmen, these unusual circumstances

Caitlin Clark

proved disorienting. Clark, however, seemed to find focus in the chaos.

"Basketball is basketball," she shrugged when asked about playing in empty arenas. "The court is still 94 feet. The basket is still 10 feet high. Everything else is just noise."That mental fortitude translated to staggering consistency. Clark scored 20+ points in 12 consecutive games during one midseason stretch. She recorded five 30-point games before February. Her assist numbers—often overlooked amid her scoring exploits—ranked among the nation's best, showcasing a playmaker's vision that complemented her scorer's mentality.

By February, national media attention intensified. ESPN featured her in multiple segments. Sports Illustrated wrote a profile titled

Caitlin Clark

"The Freshman Phenomenon." Social media clips of her logo three-pointers and behind-the-back passes accumulated millions of views. In a season where women's basketball struggled for visibility amid pandemic restrictions, Caitlin Clark became must-see TV.

"People tune in to watch greatness," explained Iowa coach Lisa Bluder. "And what they're seeing from Caitlin isn't just freshman greatness. It's all-time greatness in its early stages."

The numbers supported Bluder's assessment. Clark finished the regular season averaging 26.5 points, 6.4 rebounds, and 6.9 assists per game—statistical dominance unprecedented for a freshman in Big Ten history. She scored 644 points, breaking Iowa's single-season freshman

Caitlin Clark

scoring record by more than 200 points. Her 116 three-pointers established a new school record regardless of class.But perhaps most tellingly, she had transformed Iowa basketball. A program picked to finish fifth in the Big Ten surged to a 15-8 record and a NCAA Tournament berth. Television ratings for Hawkeye games doubled, even without fans in attendance. Practice jerseys bearing Clark's number 22 became coveted items on campus.The postseason brought new pressures and brighter spotlights. In her NCAA Tournament debut against Central Michigan, Clark delivered a triple-double: 23 points, 12 rebounds, 11 assists—becoming the first freshman to record a triple-double in the tournament since 2012. Though Iowa's tournament run ended in the Sweet Sixteen against UConn, Clark's 21 points against the

Caitlin Clark

perennial powerhouse confirmed what many already believed: a new star had arrived in women's basketball. The accolades followed: unanimous Big Ten Freshman of the Year, First Team All-Big Ten, Second Team All-American. Clark became the first freshman to lead the nation in scoring in NCAA Division I women's basketball history. Beyond awards, though, she had accomplished something more significant—she had put women's basketball on SportsCenter, had casual fans discussing women's hoops, had young girls across the Midwest practicing logo trees on playground courts.

As the basketball world caught its breath from Clark's freshman whirlwind, a tantalizing question emerged: If this was just the beginning,

Caitlin Clark

what might the future hold? The logo threes, no-look passes, and fourth-quarter takeovers had established her as a singular talent. But as her sophomore season approached, Caitlin Clark stood on the verge of something even more remarkable—transcending her sport and becoming a cultural phenomenon whose impact would extend far beyond the hardwood courts of Iowa City.

Caitlin Clark

5: The Face of the Game – Transforming Women's College Basketball

Fall 2021 arrived in Iowa City amid a buzz that transcended basketball. As students returned to campus, conversations in coffee shops, dormitories, and lecture halls inevitably circled back to one subject: Caitlin Clark. Her sophomore season hadn't yet begun, but expectations had already reached a fever pitch. Season ticket sales for women's basketball—historically dwarfed by the men's program—had surged 128 percent. National media outlets that had rarely covered Iowa women's hoops now assigned beat reporters

Caitlin Clark

specifically to track Clark's sophomore campaign.

What nobody could have anticipated was how thoroughly she would exceed even these outsized expectations.

Opening night against New Hampshire provided an immediate statement. With scouts from eight WNBA teams watching from the stands—unprecedented for an early-season non-conference game—Clark delivered a performance that bordered on mythological: 35 points, 7 rebounds, 11 assists, including a half-court buzzer-beater that left Carver-Hawkeye Arena in disbelieving rapture.

Caitlin Clark

"I remember thinking, 'We're witnessing something historic,'" recalled longtime Iowa sports columnist Chad Leistikow. "Not just a great player having a great game, but someone actively reshaping what we thought was possible in women's basketball."

The transformation was visible everywhere. Home games are now routinely sold out. Students lined up hours before tipoff, many wearing shirts bearing Clark's image or her signature shooting pose—arms extended, wrist flexed, a defender hopelessly out of position in the background. ESPN adjusted broadcast schedules to feature Iowa games in prime slots. Even opposing coaches, typically reticent to praise individual opponents, spoke of Clark with a mixture of frustration and awe.

Caitlin Clark

"You prepare for her like you prepare for no one else," admitted Maryland coach Brenda Frese after Clark torched the Terrapins for 42 points in February. "You show your team film, you design specific coverages, and then she comes out and does things that aren't even in the scouting report. She's playing a different game than everyone else."

What made Clark more than just a scoring prodigy was her comprehensive impact. Against Michigan State, she recorded the rare points-assists double-double with 31 points and 19 assists—the latter breaking Iowa's single-game record. Against Penn State, she tallied her second career triple-double. When Indiana employed a box-and-one defense

Caitlin Clark

designed specifically to contain her, Clark calmly picked it apart with 10 first-half assists before exploding for 23 second-half points when the Hoosiers abandoned the strategy.

Off the court, Clark's influence expanded exponentially. Her social media following ballooned past one million—unprecedented territory for a female college athlete not competing in gymnastics or swimming. When the NCAA finally permitted athletes to profit from name, image, and likeness (NIL) rights, Clark became an immediate beneficiary, signing deals with Hy-Vee, Nike, and Bose within weeks.

"What made Caitlin different from other athletes in the new NIL landscape was her authenticity," explained sports marketing executive Molly

Caitlin Clark

Carter. "Companies weren't just buying her talent; they were buying her genuine love of the game and her connection to Iowa. She wasn't manufactured—she was organically magnetic."

That authenticity manifested in unexpected ways. After home games, Clark often spent an hour signing autographs for young fans. Local elementary schools reported girls' basketball participation had doubled since her arrival at Iowa. When a third-grader's "Caitlin Clark Day" project went viral, Clark surprised the girl at school, creating a moment that generated more social media engagement than anything in Iowa athletics history.

National media attention reached unprecedented levels. Clark appeared on the cover of Sports

Caitlin Clark

Illustrated in January 2022. Good Morning America featured a segment on how she was inspiring young girls. The New York Times published a front-page sports story titled "The Shooter Changing the Game," complete with analytics on how Clark's range was forcing teams to defend spaces previously considered safe.

"She's not just a great college player," ESPN analyst Rebecca Lobo declared during a broadcast. "She's actively changing how women's basketball is played and perceived. That's rarefied air for anyone, let alone a sophomore."

With increased visibility came increased scrutiny. Opposing student sections targeted

Caitlin Clark

Clark with intensity previously reserved for men's stars. Online critics dissected her every gesture, questioning her occasional emotional reactions or competitive fire. Clark handled the attention with remarkable poise for a 20-year-old, neither retreating from the spotlight nor allowing it to distract from her development. "The criticism doesn't bother me," she told a reporter midway through the season. "If people are talking about me, they're talking about women's basketball. That's a win regardless of what they're saying."

By February, Clark's statistical dominance had become almost mundane in its consistency. She led the nation in scoring (27.4 points per game) and ranked second in assists (8.2), a combination unprecedented in women's college basketball

Caitlin Clark

history. More tellingly, television ratings for Iowa games had increased 86 percent year-over-year, with their matchup against Michigan drawing the largest audience for a regular-season women's college basketball game in over a decade.

The postseason spotlight burned even brighter. In the Big Ten tournament, Clark averaged 32 points across three games, including a semifinal masterpiece against Nebraska where she scored 41 points on just 20 shots. When Iowa secured a 4-seed in the NCAA Tournament, the storyline wasn't about Iowa's positioning but about Clark's potential tournament run.

That tournament produced moments that transcended the sport. Her between-the-legs

Caitlin Clark

dribble and step-back three against Creighton became an instant viral highlight. Her 35-point performance against Colorado—which included a no-look, behind-the-back pass that left even NBA stars tweeting in admiration—trended nationwide. Though Iowa's run ended in the Sweet Sixteen, Clark had firmly established herself as not just a basketball star but a cultural phenomenon.

"What we're witnessing isn't just athletic greatness," wrote Sports Illustrated's Pat Forde. "It's the rare convergence of generational talent with perfect timing. Clark arrives precisely when women's basketball was ready for a crossover star, when social media could amplify her magic, when barriers between men's and women's sports were finally eroding."

Caitlin Clark

As her sophomore year concluded, Clark had accumulated accolades that would constitute a complete career for most players: Consensus First-Team All-American, Big Ten Player of the Year, Naismith Trophy finalist. But these individual honors told only part of the story. The true measure of her impact lay in the packed arenas, the surging television ratings, the young girls now shooting from "Clark range" on playgrounds across America.

Women's college basketball had seen transcendent talents before—from Cheryl Miller to Diana Taurasi to Breanna Stewart. But none had captured the national imagination quite like the ponytailed sharpshooter from Iowa. As attention turned toward her junior season,

Caitlin Clark

basketball fans braced for what seemed inevitable: record-breaking performances, growing cultural impact, and the kind of rivalries and marquee matchups that transform individual brilliance into sporting lore.

Caitlin Clark

6: Rivalries, Records, and Rewriting History

The sellout crowd at Colonial Life Arena in Columbia, South Carolina, vibrated with anticipation. Nearly 18,000 fans—the majority clad in garnet and black—created a deafening roar as Iowa and top-ranked South Carolina took the court for their December 2022 showdown. At the center of this basketball maelstrom stood Caitlin Clark, now a junior, her ponytail swinging as she went through warm-up shots with characteristic nonchalance, seemingly impervious to the hostile environment.

Caitlin Clark

This wasn't just another non-conference game. This was theater—the sport's most electrifying offensive talent facing the nation's most dominant defense, led by the imposing Aliyah Boston. ESPN had given the matchup prime-time treatment, complete with a special College GameDay broadcast. Basketball luminaries including Magic Johnson and Sue Bird had tweeted their viewing plans. Even casual sports fans who rarely followed women's basketball had circled this date.

"In twenty years of broadcasting women's basketball, I've never felt this kind of electricity for a regular season game," ESPN's Holly Rowe would later remark. "The sport had leveled up, and Caitlin was the catalyst."

Caitlin Clark

For three quarters, the game lived up to its billing. Clark shredded South Carolina's vaunted defense with deep threes and surgical passing, tallying 32 points and 8 assists. But in the fourth quarter, the Gamecocks' depth and defensive intensity prevailed, with Boston's interior dominance securing a hard-fought 74-71 victory. As the final buzzer sounded, Boston and Clark shared a moment of mutual respect at center court—two generational talents acknowledging each other's brilliance.

The loss stung, but the game represented something bigger—women's basketball seizing the national spotlight on its own merits. The broadcast had drawn 5.5 million viewers, eclipsing most men's regular-season games. Basketball icons from LeBron James to Diana

Caitlin Clark

Taurasi had live-tweeted their reactions. For perhaps the first time, a women's regular-season game had become a genuine cultural event.

"Sure, I wanted to win," Clark told reporters afterward. "But nights like this—national audience, incredible atmosphere, two great teams—this is what grows the game. That's bigger than any individual result."

This new reality—Caitlin Clark as both basketball phenomenon and cultural force—defined her junior season. Every Iowa game became an event. Road arenas sold out months in advance. Television ratings for Hawkeye games consistently tripled previous records. The media coverage intensified to nearly uncomfortable levels, with profile writers

Caitlin Clark

from outlets like The New Yorker and Time requesting access alongside traditional sports media.

Through it all, Clark's game continued evolving to unprecedented heights. Against Ohio State in January, she recorded a mind-bending 43-point, 14-assist performance that left Buckeyes coach Kevin McGuff shaking his head in disbelief. "At some point, you just become a witness to greatness," he admitted afterward. When Indiana employed an aggressive trapping defense against her in February, Clark responded with a 45-point explosion that included eight three-pointers, several from distances that stretched the boundaries of basketball logic.

Caitlin Clark

As spectacular as these performances were, they were also building toward something more tangible: history. By midseason, statistical projections suggested Clark was on pace to challenge the NCAA Division I women's scoring record of 3,527 points, held by Washington's Kelsey Plum. The chase added another layer of intrigue to each Iowa game, with graphic trackers becoming a standard feature of broadcasts.

"Records were never the goal," Clark insisted when reporters asked about the scoring mark. "Winning is. But if those things happen along the way, that's pretty cool too."

Beyond individual accolades, Clark's junior season featured the emergence of compelling

Caitlin Clark

rivalries that elevated women's basketball. Her matchups with Indiana's Grace Berger became appointment viewing for their contrasting styles—Clark's flashy brilliance against Berger's fundamental precision. The Iowa-UConn game in Portland drew a sellout crowd and national television audience eager to watch Clark duel with Huskies star Paige Bueckers, the two players most frequently compared to each other.

But no rivalry captured the public imagination quite like Iowa versus LSU and the contrasting styles of Clark and Tigers star Angel Reese. Their Elite Eight matchup in March 2023 became the most-watched Elite Eight game in women's NCAA Tournament history, with 12.3 million viewers tuning in to watch two distinctive talents and personalities clash on

Caitlin Clark

basketball's biggest stage. The game itself became an instant classic. Clark delivered a typically brilliant performance with 41 points, but Reese's interior dominance and LSU's balanced attack ultimately prevailed in a 79-72 thriller. The postgame interactions between the two stars—analyzed and debated across social media platforms for days afterward—only added to the burgeoning rivalry narrative that women's basketball had long needed.

"Great players and compelling rivalries—that's how you build a sport," explained Rebecca Lobo on ESPN's coverage. "Clark versus Reese might be exactly what women's basketball needed to reach the next level of mainstream attention."

Caitlin Clark

Indeed, the impact of Clark's junior season extended far beyond Iowa's win-loss record or her statistical achievements. TV ratings for women's college basketball increased 71% year-over-year. Social media engagement on women's basketball content tripled. Equipment manufacturers reported unprecedented demand for women's basketball shoes and jerseys—with Clark's signature shooting sleeve becoming a particularly coveted item among young players.

By season's end, Clark had accumulated 2,717 career points—putting Plum's scoring record well within reach for her senior campaign. She had also amassed 830 career assists, positioning her to potentially become the first player in Division I women's history to record 3,000 points and 1,000 assists. Beyond the numbers,

Caitlin Clark

she had helped transform women's basketball from a niche interest to a mainstream attraction, with packed arenas and prime-time television slots now the expectation rather than the exception. As her junior year concluded, Clark faced a decision that would once have seemed unthinkable: Should she declare for the WNBA draft, where she would likely be the top overall selection? Or should she return to Iowa for her senior season, with unfinished business and untouched records still on the table?

The basketball world held its collective breath, awaiting a choice that would impact not just Clark's career trajectory but the future of both college and professional women's basketball. What was undeniable was that Clark had transcended being merely a basketball

Caitlin Clark

phenomenon—she had become a cultural force whose influence extended far beyond the hardwood courts of Iowa City. Her senior season, whether in college or the pros, promised to take that influence to unprecedented heights, transforming her from star athlete to genuine celebrity whose impact would reshape women's sports for generations to come.

Caitlin Clark

7: The Cultural Phenomenon – Beyond the Court

The sleek conference room inside Nike's Beaverton headquarters fell silent as executives awaited their guest of honor. When Caitlin Clark finally entered—dressed casually in jeans and a simple black top—the atmosphere shifted palpably. Here was a 21-year-old college athlete commanding the attention of one of the world's most powerful brands with the natural ease of someone twice her age. Over the next two hours, Clark didn't just participate in the meeting; she drove it, articulating a vision for women's

Caitlin Clark

basketball footwear that left veteran marketing executives exchanging impressed glances.

"She wasn't there as a basketball player seeking an endorsement," recalled Nike's VP of Global Basketball Scott Dixon. "She was there as a business partner with specific ideas about growing the women's game. The maturity was startling."

By spring 2023, Clark had transcended the traditional boundaries of collegiate athletics. The numbers told part of the story: 4.3 million Instagram followers, endorsement deals worth an estimated $3.1 million annually, a social media engagement rate that outpaced most professional athletes across all sports. But numbers captured only the outline of Clark's cultural impact. The substance lay in how she

Caitlin Clark

had become, almost overnight, much more than an extraordinary basketball player—she was now a brand, a voice, and a movement.

The transformation had been accelerated by the NCAA's seismic policy shift on Name, Image, and Likeness (NIL) rights, which finally permitted college athletes to profit from their fame. For most athletes, NIL represented a welcome opportunity for modest supplemental income. For Clark, it opened floodgates to corporate America's most coveted partnerships.

Within months, her portfolio included Nike, Gatorade, State Farm, Topps Trading Cards, and Buick—blue-chip brands that rarely invested heavily in women's collegiate sports. More telling than the partnerships themselves was Clark's approach to selecting them. She declined

Caitlin Clark

numerous lucrative offers that didn't align with her values, including a seven-figure deal with a fast-food chain that didn't meet her standards for nutrition messaging to young athletes.

"I'm thinking long-term," she explained to her family when turning down the offer. "What I represent matters more than a quick payday."

This discernment reflected Clark's growing awareness of her platform. As her visibility expanded, she increasingly used her voice on issues beyond basketball. She became an outspoken advocate for gender equity in sports, pointedly highlighting discrepancies in tournament facilities during March Madness. When asked about Iowa's legislative ban on transgender athletes in women's sports, she offered a nuanced response advocating for

Caitlin Clark

inclusion while acknowledging competitive complexities—earning both praise and criticism but demonstrating a willingness to engage thoughtfully on divisive issues.

Clark's cultural footprint expanded into entertainment and media. Her appearances on Jimmy Fallon and Saturday Night Live's "Weekend Update" segment showcased a relaxed charisma and self-deprecating humor that endeared her to audiences beyond sports fans. A cameo in a Taylor Swift music video generated headlines across entertainment publications that had never previously covered women's basketball. A Hulu documentary on her journey, "Beyond the Arc: The Caitlin Clark Story," broke viewing records for the platform's sports content.

Caitlin Clark

Perhaps most significantly, Clark's influence manifested in grassroots basketball participation. The "Caitlin Effect" became shorthand for the surge in girls' basketball enrollment across America—up 27% nationally since her sophomore season, with particularly dramatic increases in the Midwest. Youth coaches reported a new phenomenon: young girls practicing shots from "Clark range" and mimicking her signature step-back three-pointer.

"Before Caitlin, my daughter wanted to be a gymnast," explained Sarah Peterson, a mother from Lincoln, Nebraska. "Now she sleeps with a basketball and wears number 22 on every team. That's a cultural impact in real time."

Caitlin Clark

Television ratings underscored Clark's mainstream appeal. Iowa's games consistently outdrew major men's matchups, with their NCAA Tournament games averaging 12.5 million viewers—numbers previously unimaginable for women's college basketball. When Clark appeared on the cover of Time magazine's "100 Most Influential People" issue in April 2023, the recognition merely formalized what had become obvious: she had transcended sports to become a genuine cultural icon.

This elevated platform brought intensified scrutiny. Social media vitriol targeted Clark with disturbing regularity, often with misogynistic undertones questioning everything from her appearance to her emotional reactions during games. More substantive criticism emerged from

Caitlin Clark

within basketball circles, with some observers suggesting media coverage had become imbalanced, elevating Clark above equally deserving players, particularly women of color.

Clark navigated these complexities with remarkable poise for someone barely out of her teens. She deflected personal attacks without becoming defensive, acknowledged valid concerns about coverage disparities, and consistently redirected attention to teammates and competitors. When Angel Reese spoke about receiving less favorable coverage despite similar on-court dominance, Clark publicly agreed, noting that women's basketball needed to celebrate all its stars.

Caitlin Clark

"The goal isn't just having one player get attention," she told reporters during a Final Four press conference. "It's building a sport where many players are household names. That's how we grow the game long-term."

This maturity extended to her business decisions. Unlike many athletes who delegate their brand entirely to agents, Clark maintained active involvement in her partnerships. She insisted that her endorsement contracts include provisions benefiting women's sports broadly—like Nike's commitment to increase girls' basketball camp funding and Gatorade's pledge to expand coverage of women's collegiate athletics.

Caitlin Clark

As her junior year concluded, sports marketing experts estimated Clark's potential lifetime earning power in the hundreds of millions—territory previously reserved for elite professional athletes in men's sports. More importantly, she had helped normalize the idea that female athletes could be cultural powerhouses and marketing forces independent of their professional leagues.

"What Caitlin represents is the first true post-NIL superstar," explained sports economist Andrew Zimbalist. "She's writing a new playbook for athlete brand-building while still in college, and that's revolutionary for women's sports economics."

Caitlin Clark

With her senior season approaching, Clark stood at a fascinating crossroads—already accomplished beyond most athletes' dreams yet still with collegiate goals unfulfilled. The records within reach, particularly Kelsey Plum's all-time scoring mark, added statistical motivation. But the true intrigue lay in how Clark would wield her unprecedented platform during her final collegiate campaign.

What nobody could have anticipated was just how dramatically that senior season would unfold—how the combination of record chases, fierce rivalries, and unprecedented media attention would transform women's college basketball into must-see entertainment. As Clark prepared to don the black and gold Hawkeye uniform one final time, the sporting world

Caitlin Clark

braced for what promised to be not just a basketball season, but a cultural phenomenon unlike anything women's collegiate sports had ever witnessed.

Caitlin Clark

8: Senior Season and the National Spotlight

The air inside Carver-Hawkeye Arena on November 12, 2023, crackled with an electricity previously unknown to women's collegiate basketball. Every one of the 15,056 seats had been claimed months in advance. Ticket resellers reported prices approaching $1,000 for courtside views. Network television had dispatched their A-team broadcasting crew. Celebrities from Jason Sudeikis to Megan Rapinoe dotted the stands. Outside, a College GameDay set hand drew thousands of sign-waving fans before dawn. All this for a season opener between Iowa and Northern Iowa—a game that in previous

Caitlin Clark

years might have drawn a few thousand loyal supporters.

"It felt like the Super Bowl," Iowa coach Lisa Bluder would later recall. "Except this wasn't a championship. This was Game One of the regular season. That's when we truly understood what Caitlin had become."

When Clark finally emerged from the tunnel for warm-ups—her trademark ponytail swinging, her demeanor outwardly calm despite the circus atmosphere—the arena erupted in a thunderous ovation that lasted nearly two minutes. Thousands of young girls in number 22 jerseys pressed against railings, phones aloft, desperate to capture a glimpse of the player who had transformed their sport.

Caitlin Clark

The weight of expectation would have crushed most 22-year-olds. Clark had chosen to return for her senior season despite being a guaranteed top WNBA draft pick, citing unfinished business and records within reach. The decision had elevated anticipation to unprecedented levels. Iowa had been scheduled for a record 27 nationally televised games. Season tickets had sold out in 42 minutes. The university had installed additional media seating to accommodate the 187 credential requests for the season opener—more than they'd received for any women's game in program history.

Clark's response to this pressure? A casual 35-point, 17-assist masterpiece that included a

Caitlin Clark

half-court buzzer-beater to end the first half. Business as usual.

As her senior season unfolded, every game became a referendum on her legacy. The countdown to Kelsey Plum's all-time scoring record dominated broadcasts, with graphic trackers following Clark's point totals in real-time. After dropping 40 points against Maryland in January, she stood just 204 points shy of the record with ample games remaining. The milestone felt inevitable.

Yet records told only part of the story. Clark's senior campaign transcended statistics, becoming a genuine cultural moment that pushed women's basketball into the mainstream conversation. Iowa's February clash with Ohio

Caitlin Clark

State drew 3.39 million viewers—outperforming every NBA regular-season game that weekend. Her matchup against Indiana attracted celebrities from Travis Scott to Jason Momoa courtside. When Iowa visited Northwestern, the Wildcats moved the game to Welsh-Ryan Arena to accommodate demand, promptly selling out their 7,500-seat facility for the first time in program history.

"Caitlin isn't just having a historic season," explained ESPN analyst Rebecca Lobo. "She's creating a historic moment for women's sports, period. The visibility, the ratings, the cultural conversation—it's unprecedented."

Road games became particularly surreal. Opposing arenas that had typically drawn a few

Caitlin Clark

thousand fans for women's games suddenly sold out. Student sections that had previously been half-empty overflowed with energy—sometimes supportive, often hostile. At Nebraska, students arrived five hours early wearing shirts with Clark's face crossed out. At Rutgers, fans lined up around the block in sub-freezing temperatures. The Purdue game sold out in seven minutes—a program record.

Through it all, Clark maintained remarkable equilibrium, her game elevating rather than buckling under the spotlight. Against Illinois in February, she notched her eleventh career triple-double. Against Michigan, she broke the Big Ten career scoring record previously held by Ohio State's Kelsey Mitchell. And on February 15, 2024, in a home game against Michigan,

Caitlin Clark

history arrived: with a signature three-pointer midway through the first half, Clark surpassed Plum's record of 3,527 points to become the all-time leading scorer in NCAA Division I women's basketball history.

The moment provoked an emotional standing ovation that delayed the game for nearly four minutes. Plum herself had flown in secretly to witness the milestone, embracing Clark during the stoppage and symbolically passing the torch. "Records are meant to be broken," Plum told the television audience. "But changing the game—that's what Caitlin's really done."

As remarkable as her on-court performance was, perhaps more impressive was Clark's navigation of the off-court circus. The media obligations

Caitlin Clark

alone would have overwhelmed most athletes—daily interview requests numbered in the dozens, with outlets from Today to Good Morning America to 60 Minutes all seeking exclusive access. She maintained a grueling appearance schedule that included commercial shoots, charity events, and sponsor obligations, all while carrying a full academic course load.

"I don't know when she sleeps," teammate Kate Martin admitted to reporters. "The rest of us are exhausted just watching her schedule."

The pressure intensified as March approached, with Iowa again positioned as a high seed in the NCAA Tournament. For all of Clark's accolades—the scoring record, four First-Team All-American selections, three Big Ten Player of

Caitlin Clark

the Year awards—her resume lacked a national championship. As her final collegiate tournament approached, the narrative coalesced around one question: Could Clark cap her historic career with the ultimate team achievement?

The 2024 NCAA Tournament became, for all practical purposes, the Caitlin Clark Invitational. Television ratings shattered previous records, with Iowa's games averaging 14.2 million viewers—numbers typically associated with major professional sports championships, not collegiate women's basketball. Each game brought new drama and new viewership heights, culminating in an Elite Eight matchup against LSU that drew a staggering 16.1 million

Caitlin Clark

viewers, making it the most-watched women's college basketball game in history.

Amid the spotlight's glare, Clark delivered performances that cemented her legacy. The 41-point, 12-assist masterpiece against Colorado in the Sweet Sixteen. The redemptive victory over LSU in their highly anticipated rematch. The Final Four thriller against Connecticut that featured a 39-point explosion and a game-winning assist. Each moment seemed specifically engineered to maximize drama and viewership, as if Clark were writing her own Hollywood script.

As her collegiate career neared its conclusion, the basketball world collectively held its breath. Clark had already broken virtually every

Caitlin Clark

meaningful record, and had already transformed how women's basketball was consumed and perceived. The only question remaining was how her collegiate story would end—and what would come next as she prepared to take her talents to the professional ranks, where an entirely new set of challenges and opportunities awaited.

Caitlin Clark

9: Going Pro – WNBA and the Next Chapter

April 15, 2024. The night had finally arrived. Caitlin Clark sat beside her family in New York, a familiar nervousness churning in her stomach—the kind that had accompanied every major milestone in her life. But this wasn't just another game day. The WNBA Draft represented the culmination of a lifetime of early mornings, late nights, and countless shots launched from her driveway in West Des Moines.

Caitlin Clark

When Commissioner Cathy Engelbert stepped to the podium and announced, "With the first pick in the 2024 WNBA Draft, the Indiana Fever selected Caitlin Clark from the University of Iowa," the moment felt both inevitable and surreal. As Clark embraced her parents, tears streaming down her face, the weight of expectation settled on her shoulders. She wasn't just another top pick—she was the most scrutinized rookie in the history of women's professional basketball.

"I've been preparing for this my whole life," Clark told reporters afterward, her voice steady despite the emotion of the evening. "But I know this is just the beginning."

Caitlin Clark

The transition from college superstar to professional rookie proved more challenging than even Clark had anticipated. Her first weeks with the Fever were a brutal awakening. The speed of the professional game caught her off guard; defenders were quicker to close out on her signature logo shots, and the physicality left her bruised after practices. Even her passing lanes, which had seemed so clear in college, narrowed against WNBA veterans who had seen every trick.

In her professional debut against the Connecticut Sun, Clark struggled, shooting just 3-for-11 from the field. Social media erupted with hot takes questioning whether the college phenom could translate her game to the pros. "Welcome to the real world," one veteran player reportedly

Caitlin Clark

whispered after blocking one of Clark's three-point attempts.

Clark had faced doubters before, but never at this scale. For the first time since her freshman year at Iowa, basketball wasn't coming easily. After a particularly rough practice in late May where she turned the ball over seven times during scrimmages, Clark remained on the court long after her teammates had departed. For two hours, she ran through her shooting routine, occasionally glancing at the empty seats that would soon be filled with fans who had paid premium prices to see her perform.

"I've never been one to run from pressure," Clark told her coach that evening. "I just need to remember who I am."

Caitlin Clark

The turning point came in mid-June against the New York Liberty. Down three with eight seconds remaining, Clark waved off the designed play, crossed over her defender at half-court, and launched a shot reminiscent of her Iowa heroics. The ball hung in the air seemingly forever before swishing through the net, sending the game to overtime where the Fever would eventually secure the win. The look on Clark's face—part relief, part vindication—said everything. She belonged.

What followed was a remarkable adjustment period where Clark began adapting her game to the professional level while maintaining the audacious creativity that had made her a household name. Her assist numbers climbed as

Caitlin Clark

she learned to leverage the attention she drew to create opportunities for teammates. By the All-Star break, she had found her rhythm, earning a spot in the mid-season showcase where she participated in both the three-point contest and the game itself.

"What impresses me most about Caitlin isn't the shooting or the numbers," her veteran teammate explained to reporters. "It's how quickly she processes and adapts. She sees the game differently than anyone I've played with."

The second half of her rookie season saw Clark settling into her professional identity. Crowds continued to swell wherever the Fever played, with opposing arenas selling out for the first time in years. Television ratings for Fever games jumped 300%, and Clark jerseys became the

Caitlin Clark

league's top seller by a substantial margin. The "Clark Effect," as sports economists dubbed it, was transforming the business model of the entire WNBA.

Off the court, Clark navigated her growing celebrity with the same strategic approach she brought to basketball. She carefully selected endorsement deals that aligned with her values, launched a foundation focused on sports accessibility for young girls, and continued her advocacy for equality in women's sports. When a commentator suggested her popularity was merely novelty rather than substance, Clark responded not with words but with a 38-point, 12-assist performance the following night.

Caitlin Clark

By season's end, Rookie of the Year honors seemed a formality. More impressive was Clark's inclusion on the All-WNBA Second Team, a rare achievement for a first-year player. At her acceptance speech, she remained characteristically grounded.

"Individual awards are nice, but they've never been what drives me," she told the audience. "What matters is building something that lasts— something bigger than just one player or one season."

As her rookie year concluded, Clark had accomplished what many thought impossible: living up to the astronomical hype. Yet anyone who knew her understood that personal achievements would never satisfy her

Caitlin Clark

competitive spirit. The offseason would bring new challenges, new adjustments, and new opportunities to reshape her game and continue influencing basketball culture.

What Caitlin Clark had already built was remarkable. What she would continue to construct—her enduring legacy beyond statistics and highlights—would ultimately define her place in basketball history. As one chapter of her professional journey closed, another was just beginning to unfold—one where the true measure of her impact would be felt not just on the court, but across generations of athletes inspired by her revolutionary force.

Caitlin Clark

10: Legacy in Motion – Caitlin Clark's Lasting Impact

The true measure of greatness isn't found solely in statistics or highlight reels—it lives in the ripples created that continue long after the final buzzer sounds. For Caitlin Clark, those ripples had become tidal waves, reshaping the landscape of women's basketball and sports culture in ways that few athletes in history had ever achieved.

On a crisp autumn morning in 2026, Clark stood center court at a community recreation center in her hometown of West Des Moines. Around her, dozens of young girls dribbled basketballs, their

Caitlin Clark

eyes occasionally darting toward the WNBA star with a mix of awe and determination. This wasn't a photo opportunity or obligatory community service—this was Clark's passion project, a basketball clinic she had personally funded and organized during her offseason. As she moved from station to station, offering guidance and encouragement, the significance wasn't lost on those watching from the sidelines: the same courts where Clark had once been just another hopeful young player were now filled with girls who saw no ceiling to their basketball dreams.

"When I was growing up, I had to imagine what was possible," Clark reflected later that evening. "These girls don't have to imagine—they can see it." The "Clark Effect" has transcended mere

Caitlin Clark

popularity to become a cultural phenomenon. Television ratings for women's basketball—both collegiate and professional—had maintained their dramatic surge even after the novelty of her rookie season faded. WNBA attendance figures reached record highs across all franchises, not just when the Indiana Fever came to town. More tellingly, investment in women's sports had increased exponentially, with new corporate partnerships, improved player salaries, and enhanced travel conditions becoming the new standard rather than ambitious goals.

Sports economists pointed to Clark as the catalyst for this market correction, but the transformation went deeper than business metrics. The stylistic imprint she left on basketball itself was unmistakable. On

Caitlin Clark

playgrounds and in high school gyms across America, young players of all genders could be seen attempting shots from distances that would have been considered reckless just years earlier. Coaches who had once discouraged such long-range attempts were now incorporating "Clark drills" into their practices, recognizing that the game had evolved.

"What Steph Curry did for men's basketball, Caitlin has done for the women's game," noted a Hall of Fame coach. "She's removed artificial limitations and expanded our imagination of what's possible on a basketball court."

Perhaps most significantly, Clark had redefined what it meant to be a female sports icon in the digital age. She had masterfully navigated the

Caitlin Clark

delicate balance between accessibility and privacy, using her platform to advocate for causes she believed in while maintaining authentic connections with fans. Her social media wasn't curated by a management team but reflected her actual personality—competitive, occasionally sarcastic, unfailingly honest. When internet trolls attacked women's sports, she didn't engage directly but instead leveraged those moments into opportunities for substantive discussion about athlctic excellence regardless of gender.The narrative around Clark had evolved as well. No longer was she described with qualifiers like "great for women's basketball"—she had ascended to that rare air where her name stood alongside the sport's most transformative figures regardless of gender. Sports historians began placing her influence in

Caitlin Clark

context with athletes like Billie Jean King, who had changed not just how their sports were played but how they were perceived and valued. In academic settings, "The Clark Paradigm" became shorthand for the convergence of athletic brilliance, media savvy, and cultural impact that defined a new generation of female athletes who refused to accept the limitations of the past. Business schools studied how her authenticity had translated into marketing gold, while sociologists examined how her visibility had changed perceptions about women's sports among younger demographics. What remained remarkably unchanged through it all was Clark herself. Despite her growing collection of professional accolades and commercial success, she maintained the same work ethic that had defined her since those early days shooting

Caitlin Clark

baskets in her driveway. Teammates marveled at her continued dedication to improvement, even after establishing herself as one of the game's elite players.

"The easy thing would be to coast on what she's already accomplished," one teammate observed. "But that's never been who Caitlin is. She's still the first player in the gym and the last to leave."

As Clark's professional career progressed, the conversation inevitably turned to her place in basketball's pantheon. Was she the greatest women's player of all time? Was such a designation even relevant anymore? The more meaningful discussion centered not on where she ranked, but on how she had permanently altered the trajectory of the sport.In a reflective moment

Caitlin Clark

during an in-depth interview following her third WNBA season, Clark offered perhaps the most revealing insight into how she viewed her own journey and impact.

"I never set out to be revolutionary," she said, her trademark confidence tempered by genuine humility. "I just played the game the way I saw it, the way I loved it. If that helped other people see new possibilities for themselves or for women's sports, that means more to me than any record or championship ever could."

The revolution Caitlin Clark sparked continues to unfold—in packed arenas, on television screens, in boardrooms, and on basketball courts where future generations discover their own relationship with the game she transformed. Her

Caitlin Clark

legacy isn't static but dynamic, not finished but continually in motion—much like Clark herself, always moving forward, eyes focused not on what has been accomplished but on what remains possible.

Caitlin Clark

Conclusion

To conclude the story of Caitlin Clark feels premature. Her journey—from the driveway courts of West Des Moines to the brightest stages in basketball—continues to unfold with each passing season. Yet as we close the pages of this biography, certain truths have crystallized about the young woman who forever altered the trajectory of women's basketball.

Some revolutionaries announce their intentions with manifestos and proclamations. Clark's revolution came in the form of no-look passes, impossible three-pointers launched from half-court logos, and a refusal to accept the invisible boundaries that had long constrained

Caitlin Clark

women's sports. Her rebellion was joyful rather than angry, expansive rather than exclusive. She didn't tear down the existing structures of basketball so much as she revealed how much larger and more spectacular they could become when freed from outdated limitations.

What makes Clark's impact so profound is how it spans multiple dimensions simultaneously. On hardwood courts, she transformed the tactical approach to women's basketball, stretching defenses to breaking points and redefining spatial concepts that had governed the game for decades. In boardrooms, she rewrote financial projections and business models, proving that women's sports could command premium media rights, sponsorship deals, and arena revenues when properly valued and promoted. In living

Caitlin Clark

rooms across America, she converted casual viewers into passionate fans, people who had never watched a women's basketball game suddenly planning their schedules around Fever matchups or women's NCAA tournament brackets.

Perhaps most importantly, in the hearts and minds of young athletes—particularly girls encountering sports for the first time—she embodied limitless possibility. The phrase "play like a girl" had once carried dismissive connotations; Clark reclaimed and transformed it into an aspiration, something to be celebrated rather than overcome.

Throughout this biography, we've tracked the singular path of an athlete whose impact

Caitlin Clark

transcended sport. We've seen how her family nurtured her competitive spirit, how coaches recognized and channeled her unique talents, how teammates orbited around her gravitational pull on the court. We've witnessed her navigate disappointments, adapt to evolving challenges, and handle the weight of expectations that would have crushed less resilient souls.

What emerges is not just the portrait of a basketball prodigy but of a cultural inflection point—a before-and-after moment in the continuing evolution of women's sports. There was women's basketball before Caitlin Clark, and there is women's basketball after her. The dividing line is clear and unmistakable.

Caitlin Clark

As we step back from this biographical journey, several questions linger. How high will Clark's professional ceiling ultimately reach? Which records—once thought unassailable—will fall to her relentless pursuit of excellence? What new generations of players will emerge, inspired by her example but determined to forge their own revolutionary paths? How will history ultimately measure her contribution to the sports landscape?

These questions remain unanswered because Clark's story refuses convenient closure. Even as this book finds its place on shelves, she continues to add new chapters on courts across America, continues to challenge preconceptions about what women athletes can achieve,

Caitlin Clark

continues to expand the boundaries of her sport and her influence within it.

What we can say with certainty is this: Caitlin Clark didn't just change basketball—she changed how millions of people perceive, value, and engage with women's sports. She elevated the conversation beyond comparative metrics to one of inherent worth and excitement. She made the revolutionary act of a woman excelling in her sport feel not just acceptable but essential to our cultural conversation.

In the final analysis, Clark's most enduring legacy may not be captured in statistics or championship banners but in the fundamental shift in perspective she inspired. She taught us to value women's sports not through the lens of

Caitlin Clark

men's athletics but as their own spectacular showcase of human potential. She reminded us that revolutions don't always announce themselves with grand pronouncements—sometimes they arrive in the form of a ponytailed point guard from Iowa, pulling up from the logo, and daring us all to think bigger.

The revolution Caitlin Clark started isn't finished. In many ways, it's only just beginning. And whether she's on the court or eventually moves beyond it, the momentum she generated will continue long after the final whistle of her playing career. That might be the most revolutionary achievement of all—creating a movement so powerful that it no longer requires her presence to sustain it.

Caitlin Clark

For now, though, Caitlin Clark remains very much present, very much at the center of the basketball universe she expanded. The story continues, the revolution persists, and we remain fortunate witnesses to basketball's transformative force—the girl from Iowa who showed us that limitations in sports were always more imagined than real, and that the most important boundaries are the ones we have the courage to break.

Made in the USA
Monee, IL
20 May 2025